A CENTUM BOOK 9781910114568

Published in Great Britain by Centum Books Ltd

This edition published 2015
2015 © Universal Studios Licensing LLC.

1 3 5 7 9 10 8 6 4 2

Centum Books Ltd, Unit 1, Upside Station Building, Solsbro Road, Torquay, Devon, TQ2 6FD, UK

books@centumbooksltd.co.uk

CENTUM BOOKS Limited Reg. No. 07641486

A CIP catalogue record for this book is available from the British Library

Printed in China

ANNUAL 2016

centum

CONTENTS

Welcome to

A prehistoric world of adventure is waiting for you on Isla Nublar, and these pages are crammed with amazing facts and cool dino activities. But first we want to know a bit more about you. Fill in your details and get ready for some dino-sized fun!

Name _____

Age _____

Hometown _____

School _____

Best friend _____

Pets _____

Favourite carnivore _____

Favourite herbivore _____

Keep your eyes peeled!

After a mix-up in our labs, some of our dino eggs have been muddled up. Look out for the eggs in the pages of this book and collect the letters on them in this test tube.

When you have found all the missing eggs, rearrange the letters to find the name of one of Jurassic World's dinos.

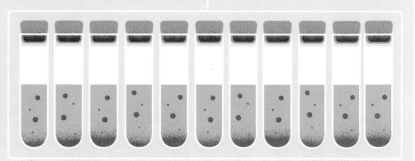

Answers on page 76

Count the Herd

It's a ranger's job to make sure that all the dinos are where they should be.
Count how many Gallimimus are in this herd.

_____

Answer on page 76

One of our visiting journalists has written an article about Jurassic World, but the computer has jumbled up the text.
Can you fill in the missing words?

Apatosaurus

big

Costa Rica

cretaceous cruise

golf course

Gyrosphere

Isla Nublar

lagoon

Mosasaurus

T. rex

theme park

Triceratops

Dr John Hammond was a man who thought big. Very ____! Twenty years ago, he imagined a _____ where everyone could share the wonder of prehistoric animals. Today, his vision has been brought to life and Jurassic World is open for business.

From the gentle _____ to the terrifying _____, the dinosaurs on _____ will take your breath away. You can watch a _____ feeding in the _____, take a _____ or explore the island in the _____ . There's even a _____ to help you relax.

In this luxury resort off the coast of _____; children can ride a baby _____ in the petting zoo and all the park's animals are safely contained for the amusement of the visitors. It's an unforgettable place where modern science interacts with creatures from the dawn of time.

Book your visit today!

Answers on page 76

The Big Dino Quiz Part 1

Our challenging quiz will test every aspect of your dino knowledge to see how much you really know. First up, see if you can answer these questions about early life on Earth. What was our planet like before humans set foot on it?

1

How long ago was the Earth formed?

a. 4.5 thousand million years

b. 10 million years

c. 20 thousand million years

2

What objects have taught us about pre-human life on Earth?

a. Cave paintings

b. Fossils

c. Ancient documents

3

For a long time nothing could live on the planet because it was too …

a. cold

b. small

c. hot

4

What were the earliest life forms on Earth?

a. Fish

b. Reptiles

c. Bacteria

5

Where did the first life on Earth appear?

a. At the planet's core

b. In the sea

c. In the trees

6

Where do amphibians lay their eggs?

a. In sand
b. In water
c. In soil

7

What is a pterosaur?

a. A flying dinosaur
b. A flying fish
c. A flying reptile

8

In which period did Stegosaurus first appear?

a. Jurassic
b. Silurian
c. Triassic

9

At the end of which period did dinosaurs become extinct?

a. Carboniferous
b. Cretaceous
c. Paleogene

10

What have scientists named the period of time when the world became very cold?

a. The Frost Age
b. The Ice Age
c. The Chilled Age

Answers on page 76

Mighty Mosasaurus

Check out these fast facts about the star attraction of Jurassic World's lagoon.

Would you have guessed that this gigantic creature is related to the tiny lizards of our modern world?

Name meaning:	Lizard of the Meuse River
Type:	Marine reptile
Length:	22m
Weight:	13,608kg
Original home:	Europe
Original era:	Late Cretaceous Period (70 million years ago)
First fossil discovered:	1764 (skull)
Diet:	Fish and other sea creatures
Key features:	Strong tail, massive teeth, powerful flippers

Colour this picture of Mosasaurus bursting out of the water.

What sort of marine predator is he trying to eat with his powerful jaws?

_____

The A–Z of Jurassic World

A is for Archean
– the second geological
aeon of Earth.

B is for Baryonyx
– a fish-eating dino first
discovered in England.

C is for Carboniferous
– the geological period
when amphibians ruled
the Earth.

D is for Dimorphodon
– our huge-headed flying reptile.

E is for Edmontosaurus
– a duck-billed dino you
may spot in groups.

F is for Ferry,
which is how you'll
travel to Jurassic World.

G is for Gene
Splicing – the
technology that helped
us create Indominus rex.

H is for Dr Hammond,
who dreamed of a place
where humans could
come face to face with
dinosaurs.

I is for Isla
Nublar
– the beautiful
location of
Jurassic World.

J is for
Jurassic World
of course!

K is for King
– did you know
that 'rex' means
King in Latin?

L is for Lagoon – where you can see our impressive feeding show.

M is for **Microceratus** – a small, horned dino.

N is for Neogene – the geological period when early humans first appeared on Earth.

O is for Othnielia – we love our tree-climbing othys!

P is for **Pachycephalosaurus** – its thick head is ideal for butting.

Q is for **Questions** – make sure you ask our rangers everything you want to know.

R is for Research – our scientists are working hard to bring more incredible creatures back to life.

S is for **Suchomimus** – massive and enormously strong, this dino has a crocodile-like skull.

T is for Triceratops – one of our most popular dinos.

U is for Unknown – we still have so much to learn about our amazing dinos.

V is for **Velociraptor** – not for the faint-hearted!

W is for Water **park** – lots of splashing fun!

X is for X-rays, which palaeontologists use to look inside fossils.

Y is for Yesterday – because here at Jurassic World, we bring the past to life!

Z is for Zoo – come and meet our gentle giants in the resort's petting zoo.

Terrifying T. rex

Our awesome T. rex will shock you with its deafening roar and its vicious teeth. It's one of the best known dinosaurs of all time, and even though it's safely contained, you should never underestimate it.

Name meaning:	Tyrant lizard
Type:	Saurischian, Theropod
Length:	13.4m
Weight:	5,443kg
Original home:	North America
Original era:	Late Cretaceous Period (65 million years ago)
First fossil discovered:	1874 (teeth)
Diet:	Meat
Key features:	Teeth, clawed fingers

Footprint Finder

Copy the T. rex footprint to make sure you'll recognise it . . .

. . . and know which way to run!

Dino Phrasebook

Saurischian is one of the two basic types of dinosaur. The name means 'lizard-hipped'. All meat-eating dinosaurs are saurischians. Theropod means 'beast feet' in Greek. Theropod dinosaurs have hooked claws on their toes.

Snap!

Many dinosaur fossils have been found with T. rex bites, showing that they suffered at the claws of this terrifying carnivore. Its victims include Triceratops and Edmontosaurus.

PART 1

STORY OF THE FILM

Gray Mitchell liked anything to do with dinosaurs. Well, not liked. Loved. He had been looking at pictures of them, reading about them and playing with models of them for as long as he could remember. And now he was going to see some real ones! Together with his older brother Zach, he was going to Isla Nublar.

As the ferry sped across the waves towards the island, Gray was so excited that he was bouncing. Isla Nublar was home to Jurassic World – the best tourist destination on the planet. Gray and Zach's aunt worked there, and they were going to stay with her. At last, Gray would see some real, live, moving, chomping, stomping dinosaurs!

Aunt Claire's assistant Zara met them off the ferry.

"Your aunt will meet you at one o'clock," she explained.

She led them onto the monorail and they swooshed along through the jungle until they reached the hotel. Gray raced up to his room and flung open the balcony door. The park stretched out in front of him, beautiful and exciting. He could see the lagoon, the visitors' centre and Main Street. There was just one thing missing.

"When can we see the dinosaurs?" Gray asked.

"After you meet up with your Aunt Claire," Zara said.

Gray didn't know how he was going to wait till one o'clock!

While Gray and Zach were looking around their hotel room, their Aunt Claire was giving some business executives a tour of Jurassic World's Genetics Lab. She wanted them to invest their money in the park.

"No one's impressed by a dinosaur any more," Claire said. "These days, kids look at a Stegosaurus like an elephant at the city zoo."

Inside the lab, dinosaur eggs were keeping warm in incubators. A baby Apatosaurus broke through its shell. Scientists were drilling into amber to extract ancient DNA, injecting fertilised eggs; and loading stacks of frozen embryos into freezers.

"Our advances in gene splicing have opened up a new frontier," Claire went on, knowing that she needed to impress the executives . "We think you'll be thrilled by our first genetically modified hybrid, Indominus rex. A new species of dinosaur, built from scratch."

"And not just built," a nearby voice said. "Designed."

The group turned and saw Dr Henry Wu, a genetic scientist.

"She'll be fifty feet long when fully grown," Dr Wu continued. "Bigger than the T. rex."

"Every time we've unveiled a new asset, attendance at the park has spiked," said Claire. "Global news coverage. Celebrity visitors. Eyes of the world."

She knew that was the sort of thing the executives loved to hear.

"When will she be ready?" the woman in the group asked.

Claire smiled. "She already is."

Claire stopped off at the visitors' centre to greet Zach and Gray, but she couldn't spend long with them. She was too busy. A short time later, she was flying over the island in a helicopter with Simon Masrani, a billionaire and Jurassic World's biggest investor. They peered down at steel paddock that rose out of the jungle. It was the home of the Indominus rex.

Construction workers were still adding concrete extensions to the paddock's massive walls. Claire led Masrani into an area encased in thick glass. There were tiny cracks in the glass where the new dinosaur had tried to break out.

"I like her spirit," Masrani said, grinning.

Workers lowered a full side of beef into the paddock on a chain. A palm frond rustled. Then ... WHOOM! A clawed hand swept the side of beef into the foliage. Masrani got a glimpse of her greyish-white back.

"Think it will scare the kids?" Claire asked.

"The kids?" Masrani said. "This will give the parents nightmares."

THUNK! The skeleton of the cow hit the ground, picked clean. Masrani gulped, feeling a sudden need to double-check the safety of the paddock.

"There's an American Navy man on the island," he said. "Part of a research programme one of my companies is running. Owen Grady."

"I know who he is," said Claire. She didn't look impressed.

"His animals often try to escape," said Masrani. "They're smart, so he has to be smarter. Let him inspect the paddock. Maybe he can see something we can't."

On another part of the island, in the Raptor Research Area, Owen Grady was training four Velociraptors. It had taken a long time, but Charlie, Delta, Echo and Blue had finally started to obey his whistled instructions.

The lead Velociraptor handler, Barry, slapped Owen on the back.

"You finally did it, man!"

Just then, a slightly older man in a suit marched up to them. Vic Hoskins was Owen's boss. He'd hired him to work for InGen, the company in charge of the Velociraptor research programme. But that didn't mean Owen had to like him.

"What do you want, Hoskins?"

"A field test," Hoskins answered. "You've proven the Velociraptors will respond to commands. Let's put this research on its feet."

Owen kept walking.

"These are wild animals. You don't want them in the field."

"The military's looking to reduce casualties," said Hoskins. "Nature gave us the most effective killing machines seventy-five million years ago! And now we know they can take orders!"

Owen was shocked.

"How long has InGen been planning to sell this idea of using the Velociraptors as weapons?" he asked.

"Since the day we hired you out of the Navy," Hoskins replied. "Look around you, Owen. Every living thing in this jungle is trying to murder the other. It's the way Mother Nature refines the pecking order. Progress always wins."

"Maybe progress should lose for a change," said Owen.

Gray and Zach managed to slip away from Zara, who was supposed to be looking after them. She had tried to keep them away from the exciting stuff, but they weren't little kids. And there was one thing they were longing to see.

Inside the T. Rex Kingdom, a live goat was standing on a platform. As Gray watched, the enormous T. rex burst out of the grove of redwood trees and devoured the goat. The crowd squealed in horror and excitement.

Gray felt sorry for the goat, but he loved seeing the T. rex. This was more like it!

Owen was working on his vintage Triumph Scrambler motorcycle when Claire drove up to his bungalow.

"I need you to take a look at something," she said. "We have a dinosaur – a new species."

Owen raised his eyebrows.

"You just went and made a new dinosaur?"

"It's kind of what we do here," Claire said, exasperated. "Mr Masrani wanted me to consult with you."

Owen kept working on his motorcycle.

"Why me?" he asked.

"I guess Mr Masrani thinks since you're able to control the raptors, you might have insight into this asset —"

"Asset?" Owen repeated, wiping grease off his hands. "You don't even act like they're alive. You may have made them in a test tube, but they don't know that."

Claire didn't like being lectured. She turned and walked back to her car. Shaking his head, Owen followed her.

Meanwhile, Gray and Zach had arrived at the Mosasaurus feeding show in the lagoon.

"The Mosasaurus is thought to have hunted near the surface of the water," said the announcer. "It preyed on anything it could sink its teeth into."

A huge shark carcass was hanging from a cable over the centre of the lagoon. An enormous swell formed in the water and the crowd rose to its feet. Then the Mosasaurus exploded straight up out of the water and grabbed the shark in its massive jaws. It crashed back into the water, soaking the crowd with a gigantic wave! People screamed in delight.

Zach and Gray looked at each other and burst into laughter.

"That was pretty good," Zach admitted. "Want to see something else cool?"

At the Indominus rex paddock, Owen couldn't see anything.

"What's this hybrid dinosaur made of?" he asked.

"The base genome is T. rex," Claire said. "The rest is classified."

"How long has the animal been in here?" Owen asked as a crane lowered food into the paddock.

"All its life. Is there a problem with our methods?"

"Animals raised in isolation, without parents, aren't always the most functional," said Owen.

The paddock supervisor was checking the infrared monitors. He couldn't see the Indominus in the paddock. Worse still, there were long claw marks on the inside of the paddock door.

"Oh boy …" he said.

It looked as if something had climbed up the door … and escaped!

One of our armoured dinosaurs, this is the largest-known member of the ankylosaurid family. It might look fierce, but don't worry – its famous tail club is only for defence.

Name meaning:	Fused lizard
Type:	Ornithischian, Thyreophoran
Length:	9.6m
Weight:	5,443kg
Original home:	North America
Original era:	Late Cretaceous Period (65 million years ago)
First fossil discovered:	1906 (incomplete skeleton)
Diet:	Plants
Key features:	Tail club, armour

You will need Troodon-vision to find all **twenty** words in this gigantic grid.

```
E F G O R T E N D S G F B S B O I S T M N O D O N A R E T P
I O E G E G J D E A C D A G E H M W I W N S P C V K L I A B
F B M S D B K S D I M O R P H O D O N T U I P W P D E C M N
R G R E G U Q K P D C B Y W T H Y K P I C S C F X G H N M S
Y F R W T R I C E R A T O P S S F A G N O U G R G Y B A C B
A P Q V S R S B E V Y M N R I T S U G K O L L S C R V U R N
G A L L I M I M U S E F Y A T U E U N Y A V T E W O I N H E
A I X S N T F A I D O D X D R K X G I G T D P L F S S T L S
Z A I S L N O L C L S H K U F I O J O N Y H N O T P A U F D
L N E H F L L D F A J Y A N X Y L T N S A S E H D H I H W A
O G H N E M S S L H N S K I P S P D M L A H I B U E T S D N
Y F U S L T N Z D M O T V S S O G H O M K U M F G R G L F U
E S O H P N E R T T H Z H U A U R S T G I K R P P E O D Z X
S Q D S I O P C A B E Y P O F G A L K M V D I U S F E E O L
V E G Q T P V P E T E P T I S U D E I Y E A O N S E T N M P
R I O Y E J A O O R A C R C R A U M C T G D I E U F E T I O
Z W O D T U A R S U G R P U T R U T C O I C E N R I H D L B
D H E U I T W P A W O R S P M I C R O C E R A T U S L R E I
C P M J T R I K S S U O P H F W X N U T E Y D K A X M B W S
S W E E D I O T Y R A N N O S A U R U S R E X P S N V X S B
R P Y E S U E E C M P U I E R T K Q W S D X K O A K P U U M
A N K Y L O S A U R U S R H D W V B C N M I O T S R M D S E
L U S A C W E R P O V E E O O J E E E P E W F B O I M I Y K
B D W F T Y J C N X Q B N M L R W C E R F R Z Y U M T Q E B O
U B M N T Y Y A U W I C E P E O I O U L V E U O N M I O R P
N S Y T W B C X N M O P L N F R P E H S G P H W O T E O T R
A T F E H L E P T E B W Y M R Q P H K W V C O R S F L C B M
L A G O O N C X N M R R H U I E P O U P U I W R E S T I R E
S R T V Y I M T C T W Q U P S U R U A S O T N O M D E R P Y
I G N M C O U E E D R W K Y R I U R G P R V W F N T U K S E
```

Ankylosaurus ✓	Apatosaurus	Baryonyx	Dimorphodon
Edmontosaurus	Gallimimus ✓	Gyrosphere	Isla Nublar
Metriacanthosaurus	Microceratus	Mosasaurus	Pachycephalosaurus
Parasaurolophus	Pteranodon	Stegosaurus	Suchomimus
Tyrannosaurus rex	Volcano	Lagoon ✓	Triceratops

Answers on page 76

Shadow Match

Can you name them all?

Match the silhouettes to their owners and then follow the instructions to make a unique shadow-box picture.

1

2

3

4

5

6

1

A

_____

C

_____

E

_____

G

7

8

_____

Shadow-box Picture

B

D

F

H

Materials

Tracing paper   Pencil

Black card   Scissors

Shoebox lid   PVA glue

Ferns, leaves, grass, bark
and other natural materials

Ask an adult to help you when using scissors.

Instructions

1   Go on a nature walk to collect your materials.

2   Trace or copy your favourite dinos onto black card and cut them out.

3   Use your dinos, ferns and leaves to form a prehistoric scene.

4   When you are happy with your design, use glue to create it inside the box lid.

5   Leave it to dry and then stick it in pride of place on your wall!

Answers on page 76

T

Make and Do: Dinosaur Mask

Create your own masks and bring your favourite dinosaurs to life right now. **Bigger teeth! Louder roars!**

Materials

Scissors • Elastic string • Hole punch
Hole reinforcers • Colouring pens or paints and paintbrushes

Instructions

1 Cut out your T. rex mask from the card pages.

2 Colour it in using realistic colours.

3 Use your hole punch and reinforcers to make holes as marked on the template.

4 Thread elastic string through the holes and tie it in place to fit your head.

You're a dinosaur! ROAR!

Danger Maze

Make your way through the Jurassic World complex to reach the ferry landing without running into a raptor. **Keep moving!**

START

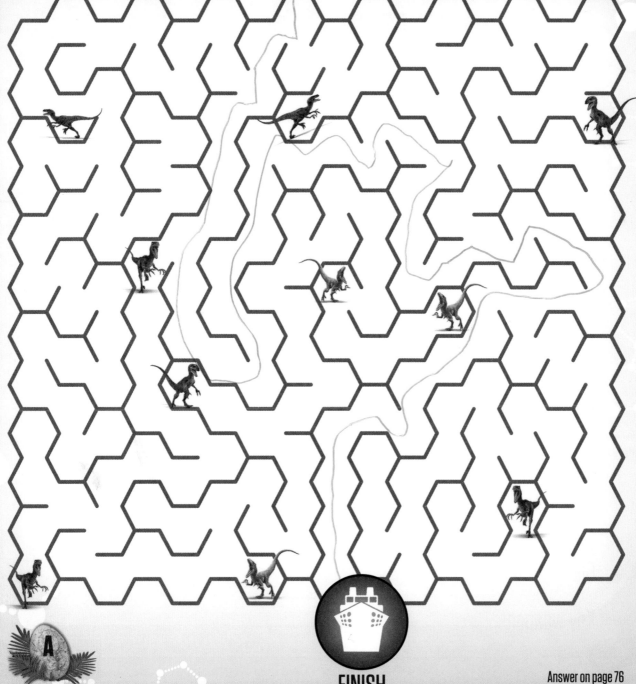

A

FINISH

Answer on page 76

Daring Dimorphodon

With its huge head,
the Dimorphodon is a
fearsome sight. It has two different
types of teeth in its mouth, which is
unusual in reptiles. Its jaw can close
extremely fast, so its victims
have to move quickly.

Name meaning:	Two-form tooth
Type:	Flying reptile
Wingspan:	2.1m
Weight:	18kg
Original home:	Europe
Original era:	Early Jurassic Period (190 million years ago)
First fossil discovered:	1828 (incomplete skeleton)
Diet:	Fish
Key weapons:	Strong jaws

Code Breaker

Use the decoder to read these fast dino facts.

1 TBUJ TWQJ WQJWNU KQVF BG JKB SWWJ.

_____ Decoded!

2 JDW ANBGJBUQMNMU GWIWN WOCUJWZ – CJ KQU Q SBUUCV TCO-MY!

_____ Decoded!

3 TBUJ ZCGB SBUUCVU QNW SBMGZ AL QTQJWMNU.

_____ Decoded!

4 JDW SCNUJ ZCGB GWUJ KQU SBMGZ CG 1923.

_____ Decoded!

5 JDW VQNEWUJ ZCGB WEEU QNW QU ACE QU AQUFWJAQVVU.

_____ Decoded!

6 JDW AVMW KDQVW CU ACEEWN JDQG QGL ZCGB LWJ ZCUXBIWNWZ.

_____ Decoded!

Answers on page 77

Amiable Apatosaurus

This large, lumbering dino is one of our favourites. The Apatosaurus is a herbivore and needs to eat more than a ton of vegetation every single day. Look out for them munching leaves in Gyrosphere Valley.

Did You Know?

The Apatosaurus's nostrils are on top of its head.

Giants on Earth

The Apatosaurus is one of the largest animals that have ever walked on our planet.

Name meaning:	Deceptive lizard
Type:	Saurischian, Sauropod
Length:	27.4m
Weight:	15,875kg
Original home:	North America
Original era:	Late Jurassic Period (152 million years ago)
First fossil discovered:	1877 (incomplete skeleton)
Diet:	Plants
Key weapons:	Tail

Footprint Finder

Looking for an Apatosaurus in the Gyrosphere Valley?
Copy this footprint so you'll know which track to follow.

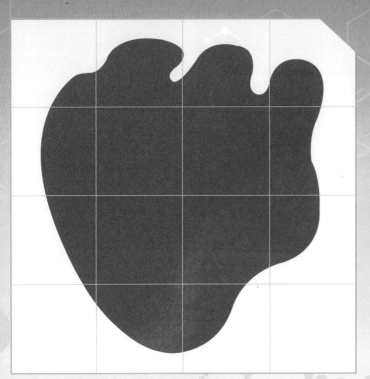

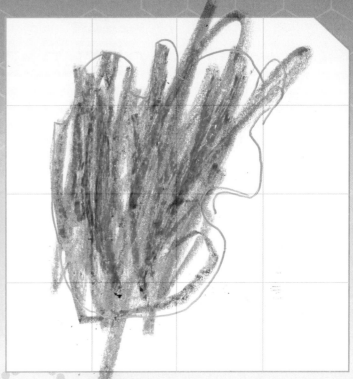

Dino Phrasebook

Sauropod dinosaurs have long necks and tails, little heads and thick, stocky legs.

PART 2

STORY OF THE FILM

In the control room, the words "CONTAINMENT ALERT" were flashing on the biggest screen. Lowery, an engineer, was on the phone to Claire. She was on her way to the control room, thinking they should be able to track the Indominus using the implant in her neck. Lowery checked the coordinates and got a shock.

"It's still in the cage," he said.

"That's impossible," Claire replied.

"I'm telling you, she's in the cage," Lowery insisted, checking the video feed from inside the Indominus paddock. "Wait. There's people in there."

Owen, the supervisor, and a worker had gone inside.

In the paddock, an urgent voice crackled over the walkie talkie.

"Paddock Eleven, this is Control. You need to evacuate the containment area."

Owen and the two other men started to run towards the security entrance, but it was too late. The massive Indominus rex snatched a worker off the ground and pushed its way out of the paddock. Owen slid under an excavator and the paddock supervisor crouched behind a

pick-up. But the Indominus flipped the truck over as if it were a toy.

"No!" the supervisor screamed.

The dinosaur tossed him in the air, chomped down and wandered away into the jungle. It was hungry … and it wanted to hunt.

In the security barracks, an alarm blared as the Asset Containment Unit prepared to go after the Indominus. Outside the Velociraptor research stables, Hoskins made a secret phone call.

"It's me. Looks like we may have an opportunity."

Owen wanted Claire to call off the ACU team. He had seen what the Indominus could do, and he knew that all those men were about to die. He realised how clever the dinosaur was. She had faked her own escape to get them to open the paddock. But no one would listen to him.

In the jungle, Captain Hamada spotted the tracking device lying on a rock. The Indominus had clawed it out. Then he felt something warm on his hand. It was a drop of blood. Then something huge moved right next to his team – something that had been hidden from sight.

"It can camouflage!" Hamada shouted. "Open fire!"

In the control room, everyone watched in horror as the heart monitors of the troopers flatlined one by one. The Indominus had killed them all.

"What have we done?" Masrani whispered.

Owen looked up at the huge screen tracking every warm body in the park. There were thousands of them.

"Evacuate the island."

"I can't," Claire said. "We'd never reopen."

"You made a genetic hybrid and raised it in captivity," said Owen. "She'll probably kill anything that moves. There's a minigun in the armoury. Send up a chopper. Use infrared to find her."

Claire shook her head.

"There are families here. I'm not going to turn this place into a war zone."

"You already have," Owen said.

He stomped out.

Claire turned and spoke to everyone in the control room.

"Okay, people, this is a Phase One, real world. Bring everyone in."

Every visitor on the island who was north of the resort area had to be brought into the resort. Immediately. Including Gray and Zach ...

Gray and Zach were in a gyrosphere, rolling between a pair of Apatosauruses. Gray laughed, loving it. Zach steered them round a Triceratops and right into the path of a lumbering Stegosaurus.

"Watch out!" Gray cried.

Zach stopped and reversed the sphere, allowing the Stegosaurus to pass. Then an announcement came through the speakers inside the gyrosphere.

"Due to technical difficulties, Jurassic World is now closed. Please disembark all rides and return to the resort."

"No!" Gray cried.

Zach looked at his brother and saw how disappointed he was.

"Come on," Zach said. "We can stay out a couple more minutes."

He put a finger to his lips, turned the volume on the speakers all the way down, and pushed the joystick forward. The gyrosphere rolled into a grove as Zach's mobile phone buzzed.

"Hi, Aunt Claire," he said.

Back in the office, Claire was pacing up and down. She had only just heard that the boys had given Zara the slip.

"Zach!" she cried in relief. "Is Gray with you?"

"We're out in the hamster-ball thing," Zach said.

"Zach, listen to me," said Claire. "You need to come back to the —"

The signal dropped abruptly, and she was cut off. Zach wasn't worried. He drove the gyrosphere up to a broken gate in the heavy wall enclosing the area. Bars twisted in all directions. Beyond the gate lay a small grove with grazing Ankylosauruses. Zach's eyes lit up.

"Dude," he said. "Off road!"

Lowery told Claire that there was one gyrosphere left in the field.

"It's going the opposite direction of where it should be going," he said.

Claire left the control room, marched through the visitors' centre and found Owen.

"I need your help," she said.

Zach and Gray rolled into a shady grove and saw four Ankylosauruses grazing.

"There," Zach said with triumph. "Up close and personal with four dinosaurs."

"Ankylosaurus," Gray said. "We shouldn't be here. And there are five dinosaurs." Zach screwed up his face and cocked his head.

"Aren't you supposed to be a genius? One, two, three, four!"

Gray pointed at a reflection in the gyrosphere's plexiglass.

"Five," he said.

Indominus rex was sprinting towards the Ankylosaurus, and the boys were caught between them. WHACK! An Ankylosaurus hit the gyrosphere with its mace-like tail. The ball flew through the air and hit a rock, the brothers hanging upside down inside it.

"We're safe in here, right?" Gray asked.

BRRZZZT! Zach's mobile phone buzzed at the bottom of the sphere.

It was Claire, calling as she climbed into a Jurassic World SUV with Owen. Zach reached for the phone.

Gray looked up and saw the Indominus staring at them from above.

"Zach . . ."

CRACK! The beast's claw broke through the glass. Its massive jaws clamped round the gyrosphere. The boys were staring down its throat. The dinosaur lifted the sphere off the ground and slammed it down onto the rocks. CRASH! The bottom of the sphere was open!

Dino Tracker

Find a die and some counters, and track a dinosaur through the park. The winner is the first player to find it without meeting a predator.
Good luck!

You join the Cretaceous Cruise. Go forward 2 spaces.

You spot Indominus rex ahead. Go back three spaces.

You hear a T. rex thumping towards you. Go forward 3 spaces.

You hitch a ride on an Apatosaurus. Go forward six spaces.

You stop at the Petting Zoo for a Triceratops ride. Miss a turn.

You are butted by a Pachycephalosaurus. Go back three spaces.

START

You spot a Velociraptor watching you from the undergrowth. Miss a turn.

A Pteranodon lifts you into the air. Go forward five spaces.

You fall into the lagoon and have to be rescued. Go back five spaces.

To cross the bridge, throw a 2 with your die.

To jump on the monorail, throw a 3 with your die.

MONORAIL

To go through the secret tunnel, throw a 5 with your die.

You catch a glimpse of the dino in the distance. Have another turn.

You drop your bag and have to return for it. Go back four spaces.

SECRET TUNNEL

FINISH

You stumble across a baby Microceratus. Sing a lullaby or miss a turn.

You try to race a Gallimimus. Go back two spaces.

GONDOLA LIFT

To use the gondola lift, throw a 4 with your die.

You lose the track and reach the volcano. Swap places with the player on your left.

FERRY

To catch the ferry, throw a 2 with your die.

Toothless Pteranodon

More fossil specimens have been found of Pteranodons than of any other pterosaur, so it was an obvious choice to join our animal community here on Isla Nublar. They are some of the largest flying animals ever known.

Name meaning:	Toothless wing
Type:	Flying reptile
Wingspan:	7.6m
Weight:	90kg
Original home:	North America
Original era:	Late Cretaceous Period (85 million years ago)
First fossil discovered:	1870 (wing bones)
Diet:	Fish
Key weapons:	Beak

The labels on our dino DNA collection have been jumbled up by a rival scientist.
Which dino does the DNA belong to?

Unscramble the letters to find out.

1

BAN ROXYY

_ _ _ _ _ _ _ _

2

STUN A
DORMOUSE

_ _ _ _ _ _ _ _ _ _ _

3

A CROCUS
TIMER

_ _ _ _ _ _ _ _ _ _ _ _

4

PROTECT AIRS

_ _ _ _ _ _ _ _ _ _ _

5

PUSH UP A
ROAR ALSO

_ _ _ _ _ _ _ _ _ _ _ _ _ _

6

SUMO IS
MUCH

_ _ _ _ _ _ _ _ _

Answers on page 77

The Big Dino Quiz Part 2

It's the second part of our monster quiz, and this time we want to know if you can recognise the amazing animals that live in Jurassic World.

1 Which 13,000kg marine reptile can be seen in the Jurassic World lagoon?

_____

2 Which dinosaur's close-up is this?

_____

3 Which flying reptile has a huge head?

_____

4 Which dinosaur's close-up is this?

_____

5 Which is the longest dinosaur living in the park?

_____

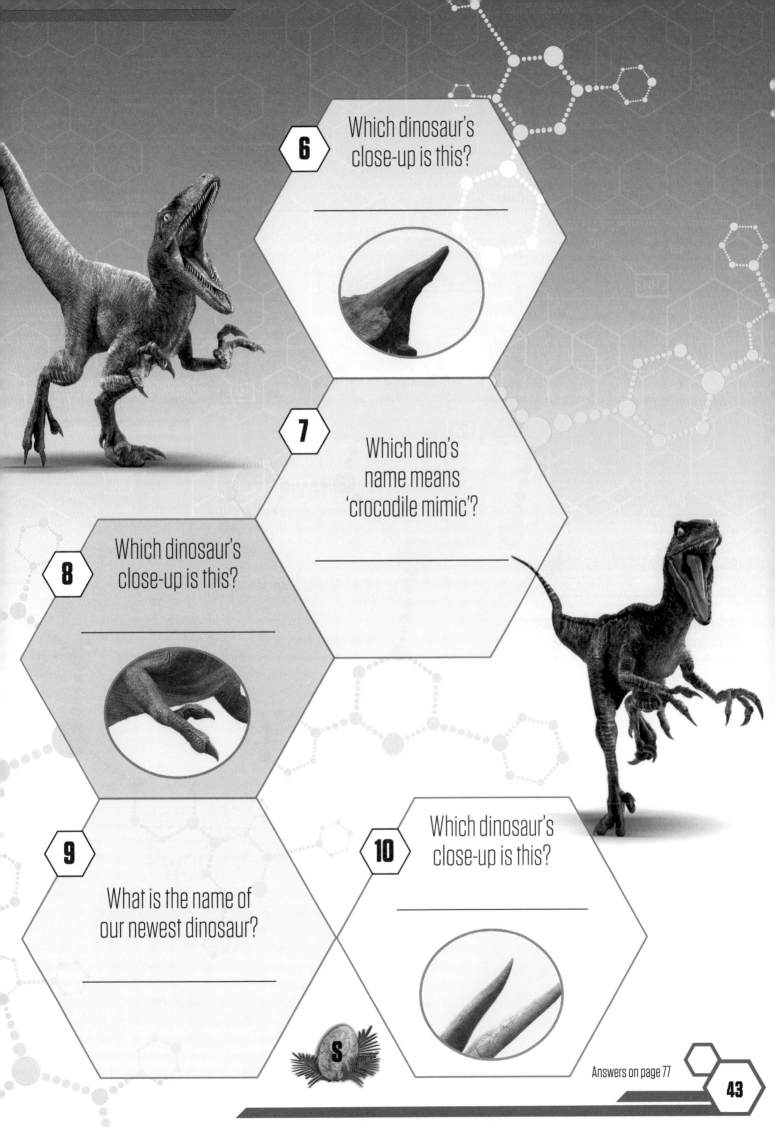

6 Which dinosaur's close-up is this?

_____

7 Which dino's name means 'crocodile mimic'?

_____

8 Which dinosaur's close-up is this?

_____

9 What is the name of our newest dinosaur?

_____

10 Which dinosaur's close-up is this?

_____

Answers on page 77

43

Vicious Velociraptor

Our raptors are some of our most dangerous predators. By the time the victim spots a raptor, it's usually already too late. They are master hunters, and they show no mercy. With its 'S'-shaped neck, a raptor can strike at its prey like a snake.

Name meaning: Swift seizer

Type: Saurischian, Theropod

Length: 3.6m

Weight: 45kg

Original home: Central Asia

Original era: Late Cretaceous Period (75 million years ago)

First fossil discovered: 1923 (skull and claw)

Diet: Meat

Key weapons: Teeth, claws

Did You Know?

The Velociraptor is a good jumper, and thanks to its stiff tail it can even change direction in mid air!

Footprint Finder

Hopefully you'll never find a Velociraptor footprint in the wild! But just in case, copy it here ...

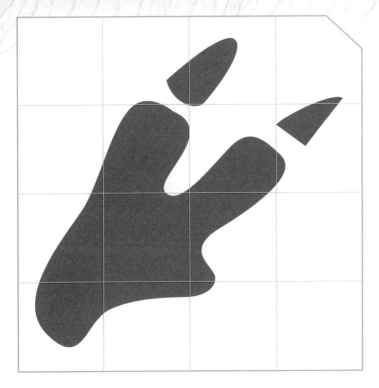

Fossil Fight

One of the most famous Velociraptor fossils shows that it died while locked in a ferocious battle with a Protoceratops.

... and make sure you never forget it!

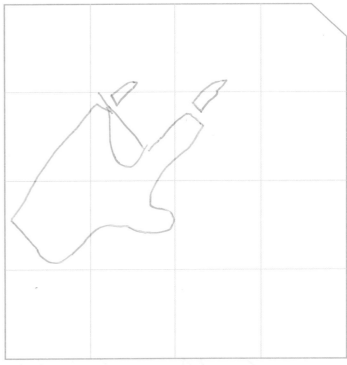

Feet

A raptor's first 'toe' is a small dewclaw, and the second is a big claw, shaped like a sickle. It can grow to over 6.5cm and it's used to capture and tear into prey. Raptors walk on their third and fourth toes, so the killing claw stays sharp and deadly.

PART 3

STORY OF THE FILM

The boys scrambled out onto the rocks. SMASH! The Indominus brought the sphere crashing down around them.

"Run!" Zach cried. "No, wait!"

Zach grabbed Gray and sheltered him with his body as the Indominus smashed the globe down around them again. It lifted the sphere once more.

"NOW! RUN!" Zach yelled.

The boys took off. The Indominus sent the broken ball flying and thundered after the boys. Zach and Gray ran through narrow woods.

"Go, go, go!" Zach cried.

"I'm going!" Gray replied, just as the Indominus crashed through the jungle behind them.

They reached the edge of a waterfall with a steep drop into a pool. The Indominus was charging up behind them.

"Jump!" Zach shouted.

SPLASH! Zach and Gray plunged into the water. The Indominus looked over the edge, snorted in frustration, and stomped off into the jungle. Gasping for breath, Zach dragged his brother onto the muddy shore. They clung together, choking on water and tears, and thankful to be alive.

Back in the control room, Lowery had been watching footage from the Indominus's paddock. He had found that the Indominus could camouflage itself from the thermal camera. It could change its heat signature.

Claire and Owen drove through Gyrosphere Valley. As they searched for the boys, they found six dead Apatosauruses. Finally they discovered the shattered remains of the gyrosphere, with a massive dinosaur tooth jammed into it. Claire's face went white when she spotted Zach's mobile phone.

"They made it out," Owen told her. "Brave kids."

He pointed to two sets of footprints leading to the edge of the waterfall, where they abruptly stopped.

"Zach! Gray!" shouted Claire.

Owen clamped his hand over her mouth.

"Those boys are still alive, but we won't be if you keep screaming like that!" he whispered.

Claire nodded. That made sense. She had to find her nephews.

Deep in the jungle, Zach and Gray found a crashed maintenance vehicle. There was no one inside. The driver's seat was ripped and stained with blood. Zach took his brother's arm.

"We shouldn't stay here," he said.

As he backed away, Zach stumbled over a staircase leading up to a vine-covered building. It was the visitors' centre that had been built for the original Jurassic Park in 1993.

The brothers pushed through the front door. Making their way through a tangle of vines, they found an old Jurassic Park jeep. Between the two broken vehicles, perhaps they could build themselves some transport.

In a small cove on the island, Hoskins arrived with a private military transport boat. It was carrying armoured vehicles and black cases marked 'InGen'. Barry was watching them from above the cove. He spoke into his two-way radio.

"Owen, we have a situation here." He heard nothing but static. "Owen, where are you?"

In the control room, Lowery was looking at the park map on a screen.

"She's headed straight for the resort," he said.

Hoskins walked in as if he owned the place.

"My team has spent two years working on an application that could hunt and kill that creature," he said.

Masrani glared at him.

"Your programme was meant to test their intelligence."

Hoskins nodded. "They can follow orders. The solution to this crisis is right in your hands."

"Let me be as clear as I can," said Masrani. "No Velociraptors are to be set loose on this island."

As Hoskins glared at him, Masrani headed out to fly his helicopter. ACU troopers were bolting a turret gun into the cabin. Somehow, the Indominus had to be stopped.

Claire and Owen were making their way through thick jungle when they heard a motor revving. They ran towards the sound, and found the old visitors' centre. The jeep was gone, but Owen picked up Zach's hoodie. Claire's nephews were still alive.

"That road'll take them straight to the resort," Owen said. "We have to get back."

But just then, they heard a thunderous footstep. Dust crumbled from the ceiling. Owen grabbed Claire and pulled her behind an old jeep. THOMMMP! THOMMMP! Through the broken ceiling, they saw the Indominus.

They raced out through the visitors' centre and slid down an embankment. Lying in the mud, they heard the Indominus thumping closer and closer. Silence. Then … WHACK! It sent a fallen tree flying down the embankment – straight towards Owen and Claire.

The tree missed their heads by inches. The Indominus peered over the edge of the embankment, growling. Suddenly Masrani's helicopter buzzed overhead. The Indominus looked up, narrowed its eyes, and raced away.

The helicopter tracked the Indominus to the Pteranodon Aviary, a domed cage of steel and glass. BOOM! The turret gun fired and hit a tree. The dinosaur ripped through the glass and metal, and crashed through the dome. Four Pteranodons stumbled out through the hole and took flight, screeching towards the helicopter.

"Bring it up!" screamed the gunner.

Masrani pulled the helicopter up, but not fast enough. WHACK! A Pteranodon hit the helicopter's spinning blade. And then another. The chopper spun and crashed through the roof of the aviary. Smoke billowed out of the aviary and the Indominus charged out. No one could possibly have survived that crash.

A massive flock of Pteranodons and Dimorphodons streamed out of the aviary through the smoke. They were confused and angry, and they were heading towards the resort.

In their Jurassic Park Jeep, Zach and Gray smashed through an old rusted gate and screeched onto a main road.

"We made it!" Zach said. "We're safe now!"

Gray looked up and saw eight massive Pteranodons flying above them. They zoomed towards a security gate that protected the resort from the rest of the island.

"Open it!" they screamed at the guard, pointing to the sky. "Open the gate!"

When Claire and Owen got back to the resort, Main Street was packed with fleeing tourists and the sky was filled with flying reptiles. Tourists ran as the reptiles dived towards them. In the petting zoo, a Pteranodon tried to carry off a baby Triceratops, but it was too heavy.

Zach and Gray found Zara and stared as Pteranodons and Dimorphodons attacked the helpless tourists.

"What's happening?" cried Zara. "What —"

WHOMP! A Pteranodon swiped her off the ground and carried her into the air, screaming. A second Pteranodon snatched her out of the other's claws. They fought over their prey, flying out over the lagoon. Then they dropped her. Zara plummeted into the water and the Pteranodons dived in after her, slicing through the water. One of them grabbed her in its jaws and swam to the surface. Then WHOOSH! The Mosasaurus exploded out of the lagoon, engulfing the Pteranodon and Zara in one gigantic bite.

While ACU workers battled the flying reptiles with electric spears and tranquilliser guns, Owen and Claire ran onto the resort's boardwalk. Zach and Gray ran out onto the other end of the boardwalk and a Pteranodon dived towards them.

"Run!" Zach yelled.

Zach shoved his brother out of the way as a Dimorphodon attacked Owen. As he struggled with it, Claire swung a rifle like a bat, cracking the Dimorphodon in the face. She fired and the reptile flew backwards.

Owen jumped up and kissed Claire. Then she saw her nephews were with him.

"Zach! Gray!"

"Aunt Claire?" Gray shouted.

They ran towards her and she pulled them into a tight hug.

Owen led Claire and the two boys through the crowds. Claire pulled out her phone.

"Lowery, I'm on my way back to you," she said.

In the control room, Lowery checked over his shoulder and ducked into a side office.

"Bad idea," he replied in a low voice. "InGen's private security division have taken over. That guy Hoskins is in charge. He's got some insane plan to use the raptors."

The InGen helicopter buzzed overhead, heading for the Raptor Research Arena on the east coast of the island. Owen, Claire, Zach and Gray jumped into an abandoned vehicle and sped off in the same direction.

At the Raptor Research Arena, Hoskins watched InGen workers unpacking military gear. The four Velociraptors were penned in steel cages. Bars hugged their bodies to keep them from attacking their handlers.

Owen drove up, jumped out of his vehicle and headed straight for Hoskins, followed by Claire and the boys.

"Get out of here and stay away from my animals," Owen ordered.

Claire and the boys came up behind him.

"This is an InGen situation," said Hoskins. "Everyone on the island will make it out safe. And if you watch the news tomorrow, you'll see a story about how we saved lives. Or to be more accurate, they saved lives."

He nodded towards the Velociraptors. Claire and Owen were silent. They knew that the people on the island had to be saved.

"This is happening," Hoskins said. "With or without you."

"If we do it," Owen said, "we'll do it my way."

Graceful Gallimimus

The Gallimimus is built for fast running, with long legs, a heavy tail base and short toes. Make sure that you take time to watch the Gallimimus flocking across the valley at top speed. It's a beautiful sight!

Name meaning: Chicken mimic

Type: Saurischian, Ornithomimid

Length: 4.6m

Weight: 200kg

Original home: Asia

Original era: Late Cretaceous Period (70 million years ago)

First fossil discovered: 1963 (incomplete skeleton)

Diet: Plants, insects, lizards

Key weapons: Legs

There are still a lot of things that scientists don't know about dinosaurs. Are you good at picking out the facts from the fiction? Five of these statements are true and five are false.

Can you guess which is which?

TRUE   FALSE

1. A Mosasaurus doesn't lay eggs.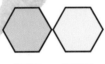

2. A Triceratops has no more than fifteen teeth.

3. Indominus rex first lived 100 million years ago.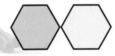

4. Stegosaurus has the largest brain of any dinosaur.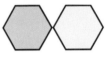

5. T. rex has a very good sense of smell.

6. Many fossils have been found showing Stegosaurus and T. rex in combat.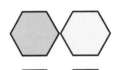

7. The first Velociraptor fossil was found in Mongolia.

8. Ankylosaurus is about the size of a chicken.

9. Gallimimus doesn't have very good eyesight.

10. Pteranodons are covered with tiny; soft feathers called down.

Answers on page 77

Dino Future?

Create your own dinosaur adventure!
Jurassic World has given you the chance to meet some amazing prehistoric animals. Now dream up a story with you in the starring role. Use the spaces to draw pictures of your most exciting moments.

Set the scene! Where are you and what can you see?

One day in Jurassic World _____

_____

_____

_____

_____

_____

_____

_____

Something shocking happens – what do you do?

Add an unexpected twist!

Will it be a happy ending?

Make And Do: Dino Maker

Instructions: How to build your T. rex model

Head

1. Press out **part 15**. Fold the sides of the head by sliding the green and purple tabs into the matching slits.

2. Then slide the tabs on the top piece of the head into the slits on the sides.

3. Press out **part 16**. Roll it into a semi tube. Slide both the yellow and dark pink tabs into the matching slits.

4. Press out **part 17**. Fold the sides and slide the light purple tab into the matching slit.

5. Slide the blue tab on **part 16** into the matching slit on T. rex's body **part 14**.

6. Now slide the long pink tab on **part 17** into the matching slit on **part 14**. Copy for the other side of the jaw.

Tail

1. Press out **part 1**.

2. Roll the end of the tail to create a cone – as it's a tight cone you may find it helpful to roll it round a pencil first.

3. Slot the tab into the slit. It helps to bend the edges of the tab down so that it holds in the slit better.

4. Do the same for the second piece of **part 1**.

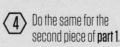

5. Create an angle in the tail by joining the two parts with the 'hook' that has been made.

6. Press out **part 2**.

7. Roll **part 2** to create a tube and slot the tabs into the slits.

8. Slot the tabs at the end of part 1 into the slits in **part 2** – match the dark pink dots first and then slide in the second tab.

 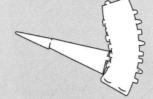  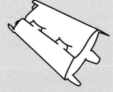 
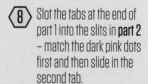

9. Fold down the edge tabs on **part 3**. Match the green dots first, then slot the tabs on **part 2** into the slits on **part 3**. Then join the ends together.

10. Add **part 4** to **part 3** in the same way as the previous step. Then add **parts 5 and 6** in the same way too – always start adding the part by matching the coloured dots.

11. This is what it should look like when all the parts are assembled.

Back Legs

1 Press out **part 7**. Roll the upper leg into a tube and slot the tabs into the slits. Bend the edges of the tab down so that it holds in the slit better.

2 Roll the lower leg and the top of the foot into tubes. Slot the top of the foot onto the tab in the bottom of the lower leg to create an angle.

3 Slot the tabs at the top of the lower leg into the slits in the upper leg to create an angle.

4 Create the top of the leg by bending the side down and tucking it behind the upper leg. Match the light blue tab and slide it into the matching slit.

5 Do the same to the other side, by sliding the dark blue tab into the matching slit.

6 Fold the bottom of the foot underneath and then fold the tabs upwards. Bend the sides of the foot downwards and slot the tabs into the slits.

7 Press out **part 8**. Fold the bottom of the foot underneath and then fold the tabs upwards.

8 Bend the sides of the foot downwards and slot the pink and purple tabs into the matching slits.

 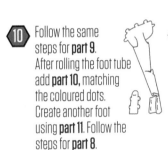 

9 Slide the bottom of the leg into the foot. Roll the back of the foot round, trapping the bottom of the leg in place, and slot the tabs together.

10 Follow the same steps for **part 9**. After rolling the foot tube add **part 10**, matching the coloured dots. Create another foot using **part 11**. Follow the steps for **part 8**.

11 Slot the two legs into the back end of the body. Slide the orange and white tabs into the matching slits on the body.

Neck and Arms

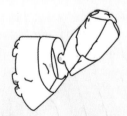   

1 Press out **part 12** and roll into a tube. Bend the edges of the tab down so that it holds in the slit better.

2 Fold down the edge tabs on **part 13**. Slide the dark blue tab on **part 12** into the matching slit on **part 13**. Copy for the other tabs and join the ends together.

3 Press out **part 14**.

4 Roll the bottom piece of **part 14** to make a tube.

5 Wrap the top piece to form a tube, slotting the two tabs into the slits.

6 Attach **part 14** to **part 13**. Slide the yellow tab into the matching slit.

7 Take **parts 18 and 19**. Fold the lower arm and thumb on both parts. Then slide them into the slits on **part 12**.

8 Now slot the front part of the body onto the back part of the body. Slide the green tab on **part 6** into the matching slit on **part 12**. When the body is joined, squeeze the tops of both legs to flatten them out – this will help your T. rex stand up.

Sturdy Stegosaurus

Slow and steady, the Stegosaurus is well defended by its plates and spikes. It's about the size of a bus, so even the toothy T. rex thinks twice about attacking!

Name meaning:	Covered lizard
Type:	Ornithischian, Thyreophoran
Length:	10m
Weight:	4,500kg
Original home:	North America and Europe
Original era:	Late Jurassic Period (145 million years ago)
First fossil discovered:	1877
Diet:	Plants
Key weapons:	Spiked tail

A

How many new words can you make from the name
of Jurassic World's newest dinosaur?

INDOMINUS REX

_____

_____

_____

_____

_____

_____

_____

_____

_____

_____

_____   _____

_____   _____

Terrific Triceratops

Triceratops is a sturdy and brave dinosaur. With its horns and frills, it's a favourite with our visitors. It has one of the largest skulls of any land animal – almost a third of the length of its entire body!

Name meaning:	Three-horned face
Type:	Ornithischian, Marginocephalian
Length:	9.1m
Weight:	5,550kg
Original home:	North America
Original era:	Late Cretaceous Period (65 million years ago)
First fossil discovered:	1887 (horns and incomplete skull)
Diet:	Low-growing plants
Key weapons:	Horns

Footprint Finder

You will be sure to recognise Triceratops tracks once you've copied this massive footprint!

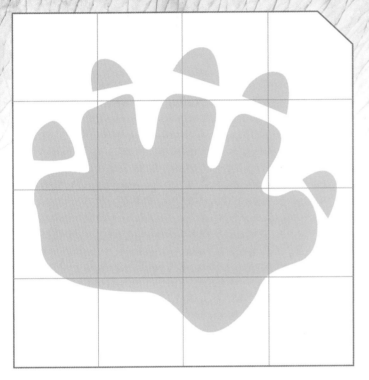

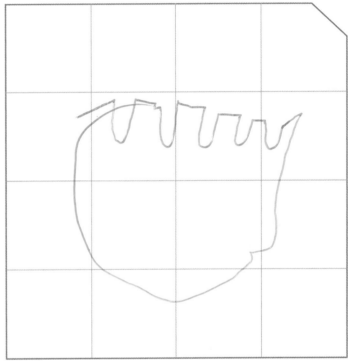

Did You Know?

It is believed that originally Triceratops lived in small family groups.

Limbs

The legs of a Triceratops need to be very strong to be able to move its enormous body. Its front legs are shorter than its back legs, and they each have five toes. The back legs have four toes each.

Teeth-tastic

Triceratops teeth are stacked in columns, so they can always be replaced. This means that they can have as many as 800 teeth!

PART 4

STORY OF THE FILM

Owen went to check on the Velociraptors. He reached through the bars of Blue's cage and placed his hand on her snout. She lightly bumped him with it. Zach and Gray came up behind Owen.

"Are they safe?" Gray asked.

"Not really," said Owen.

He explained that Blue was the beta. That meant she was second-in-command.

"Who's the alpha?" Gray asked.

"You're talking to him, kid," Owen said.

Owen used the bloodstained tracking device to give the raptors the scent of the Indominus. They bucked and screeched, eager to find the source of that blood and kill it. Owen fastened a night camera to the handlebar of his Triumph and revved the engine. Then the gates were raised and the Velociraptors raced out into the night, searching for their prey.

Owen sped along among the Velociraptors, a team of five on the hunt. They reached a clearing and the raptors slowed down. Then they reared up and backed away as the jungle moved and the Indominus came out of camouflage. Hissing, the raptors surrounded their prey. The Indominus roared, and suddenly the Velociraptors relaxed.

"Something's wrong," Owen said.

The raptors circled the Indominus, looking curious. Then Blue, Charlie, Delta, and Echo took their places at the side of the Indominus.

"Watch your back!" said Owen. "The raptors have a new alpha!"

In the Genetics Lab, Hoskins and his men were evacuating. Workers were putting their creations in emergency storage. Dr Wu stepped into a secret lab as his phone buzzed.

"Where have you been?" he said into his phone.

"Change of plans," Hoskins replied. "I need all the new assets off-site."

Claire hurtled away from the raptors in a Jurassic World vehicle, with Zach and Gray in the back.

"Drive!" Zach yelled. "Go!"

The raptors raced after them. Claire was driving as fast as she could, swerving to knock the dinosaurs out of the way. Charlie tried to jump through the doors in the back, but Zach grabbed an electric spear and he and Gray jabbed it into the raptor's chest. Charlie screeched and tumbled away, taking the spear with her.

At last, Claire, Owen and the boys made it to the visitors' centre. When they reached the Genetics Lab, they found the hidden laboratory. There were cages and tanks full of genetically modified experiments. A monkey with bat wings. A fish with clawed hands and feet.

"What is all this?" Claire said.

From the doorway behind them, Hoskins said, "I'm afraid that's above your pay grade."

The four of them spun round to face him.

"Where's Henry?" Claire asked.

"Dr Wu works for us," Hoskins said.

Hoskins told them that he wanted to create genetically modified dinosaurs as weapons. But as he spoke, he heard claws ticking on the floor. Owen, Claire, and the boys hid in the shadows as Echo peered round the corner and backed Hoskins up against a wall.

"Easy, now," he said, holding out a hand.

Echo attacked him, and Owen grabbed Claire's hand.

Claire, Owen, Zach and Gray ran back through the main lab and into the hallway. They reached Main Street with Echo and Charlie close behind. Blue lunged out of the darkness.

"That's how it is, huh?" Owen said.

Blue hissed. But she didn't attack. Owen slowly raised his hand.

"When she was born," he said, "she looked up at me, right into my eyes, like this." He raised his open hand higher. Blue recoiled.

"Easy ... easy ..."

THOOM! THOOM! The Indominus was coming. It roared and Blue backed away.

"No, no," Owen said. "Stay with me. Come on, girl."

The Indominus came stomping towards them in the moonlight, roaring to tell Blue to attack. But Blue snapped back, and the Indominus flung her aside. Charlie and Echo watched. They looked back at Owen, then up at the Indominus. Which alpha would they choose?

Echo and Charlie moved back to Owen's side, facing the Indominus in attack positions. Claire and the boys ran for cover as Owen gave the attack signal.

Charlie and Echo leapt onto the Indominus's back, digging their teeth and claws in. From

their hiding place, Claire and the boys watched the battle.

"We need more," Gray mumbled.

"More what?" Claire asked.

"Teeth," he said. "We need more teeth."

Claire grabbed a leather emergency pack and ran into the darkness. Blue and Charlie were down, leaving only Echo. A single raptor was no match for the Indominus. The massive dinosaur slammed her to the ground.

Standing outside the steel door of a paddock, Claire called Lowery in the control room.

"I need you to open Paddock Nine," she said.

Lowery pressed a button on his keyboard and the steel door rose. Claire took a flare out of the emergency pouch and lit it.

BOOM. BOOM. Footsteps thundered. Puddles rippled. The T. rex was coming. Claire ran as fast as she could, using the light of the flare to lead the T. rex on.

Further down Main Street, the Indominus was attacking Owen and the boys. Claire threw the lit flare at the Indominus and the two colossal beasts rushed at each other.

As the humans hid from the battle, Blue reappeared out of the dark. She latched her razor-sharp teeth onto the Indominus's leg. The Indominus turned and the T. rex slammed its head into the monster, which crashed backwards onto the lagoon boardwalk.

The Indominus struggled to her feet and roared, as the Mosasaurus erupted out of the lagoon. Its huge jaws clamped on the mighty Indominus rex, and dragged her deep into the water.

The T. rex lumbered off into the night and Blue disappeared into the shadows. They were free to roam the island.

Claire, Owen, Zach, Gray and all the survivors were rescued from the island. Isla Nublar no longer belonged to the humans. A small flock of Pteranodons circled overhead. The T. rex stood on the roof of the visitors' centre and roared.

The king of the dinosaurs stood its ground. It was ready for anything.

Crossword Challenge

How well do you know your dinosaurs? Well enough to complete a crossword without any clues? Every answer is the name of one of Jurassic World's dinos. Can you figure out where each one goes?

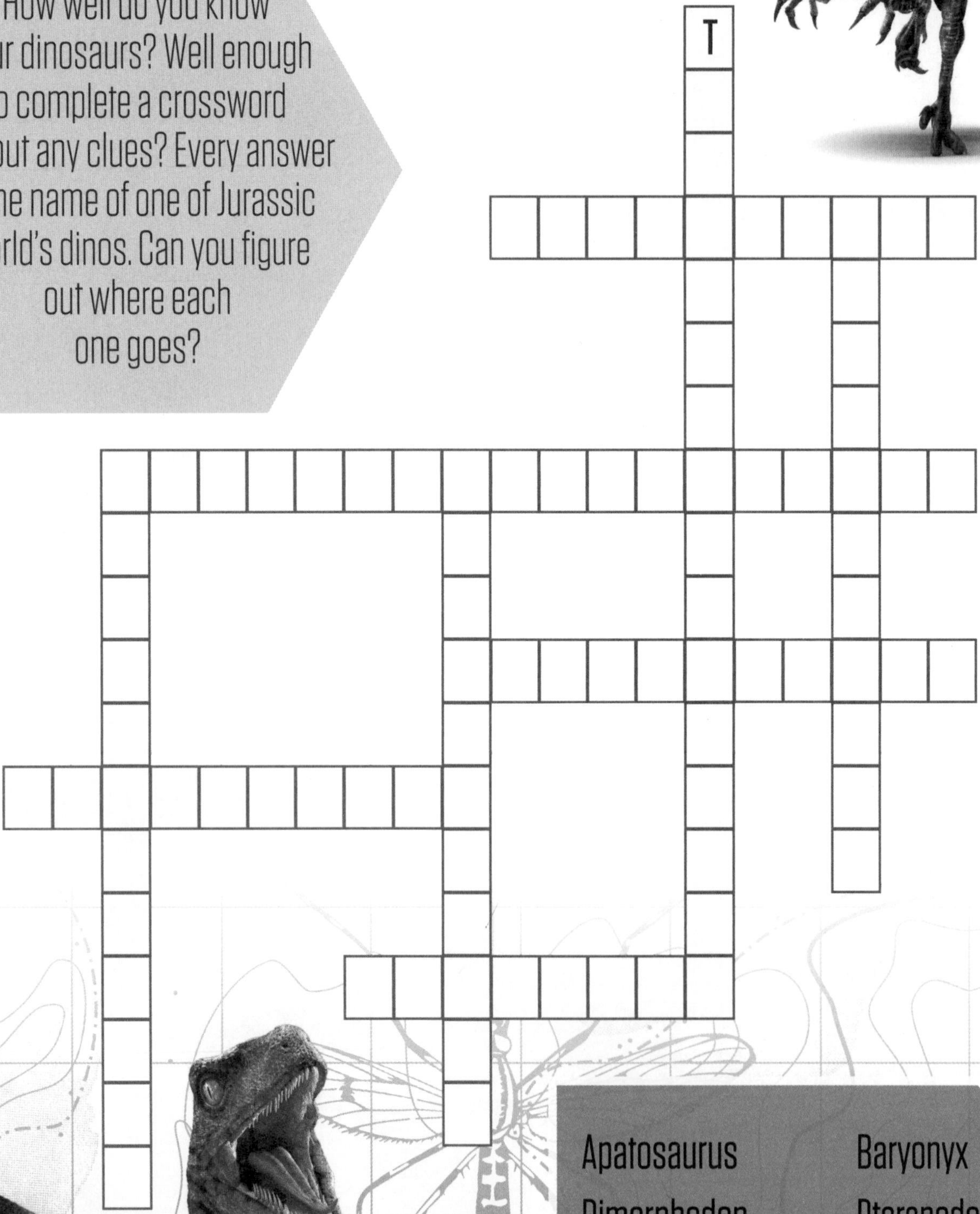

T

Apatosaurus   Baryonyx

Dimorphodon   Pteranodon

Metriacanthosaurus   Microceratus

Suchomimus   Triceratops

Tyrannosaurus rex

Answers on page 77

You're a dino expert, heading into the wildest areas of Isla Nublar to discover all the secrets of Jurassic World. What will you pack in your kit bag? Draw your gear right here.

Incredible Indominus rex

Thanks to the wonder of gene splicing, this awesome dino was created by Jurassic World scientists. It has never lived on the Earth before, so our visitors will enjoy watching as it discovers and explores its world.

Name meaning: Untameable

Type: Saurischian, Theropod

Length: 15.2m

Weight: 5, 443kg

Original home: Isla Nublar

Diet: Meat

Key features: Teeth, claws, spiked head and spine

An Epic Battle

Colour in this picture of a battle to the finish between Indominus rex and Stegosaurus.

Did You Know?

How many of these amazing dino facts did you already know?

◇ People who study dinosaurs are called palaeontologists.

◇ Pteranodon's wings are made of skin and muscle.

◇ An Apatosaurus swallows stones to grind up the food in its stomach.

◇ Dinosaurs are the ancestors of modern birds.

◇ Dinosaurs lived on Earth for more than 160 million years.

◇ The word 'dinosaur' means 'terrible lizard'.

◇ Not all dinosaurs are gigantic. Some of them are as small as cats!

◇ Most dinosaurs are vegetarians.

◇ There is a small town called Dinosaur in the United States, and many of its streets are named after dinosaurs.

◇ When dinosaur fossils were first discovered, some people thought that they were the bones of giant humans!

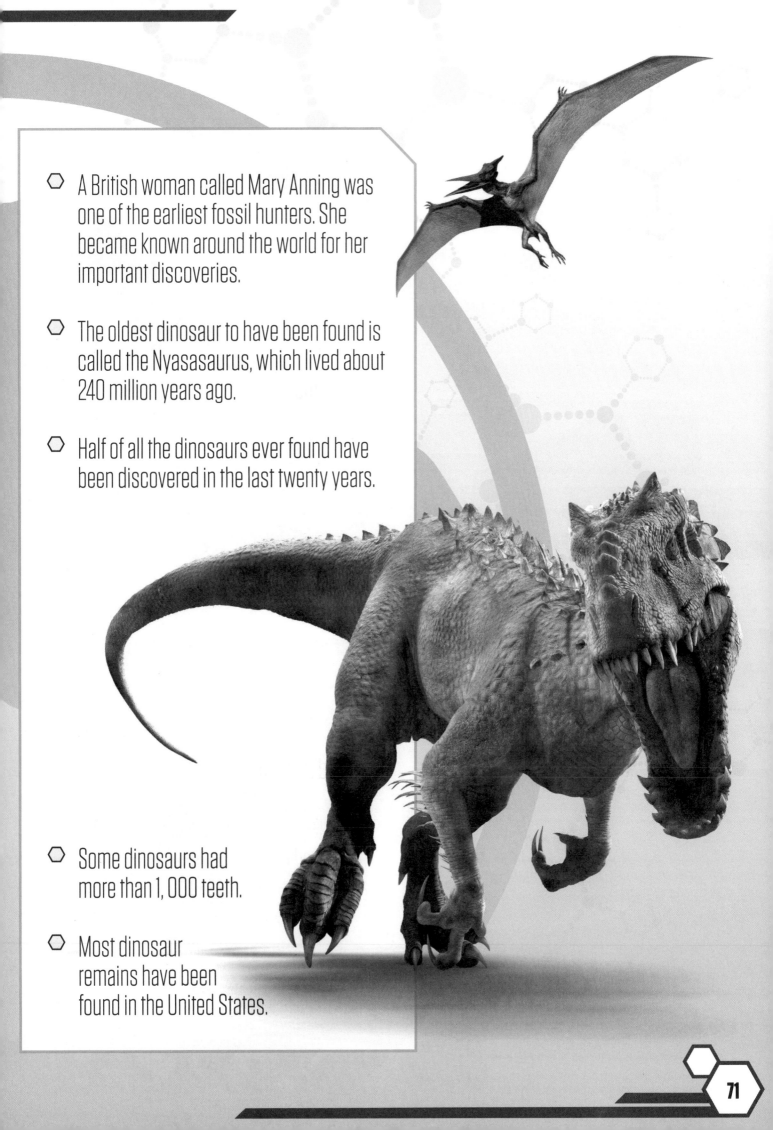

- A British woman called Mary Anning was one of the earliest fossil hunters. She became known around the world for her important discoveries.

- The oldest dinosaur to have been found is called the Nyasasaurus, which lived about 240 million years ago.

- Half of all the dinosaurs ever found have been discovered in the last twenty years.

- Some dinosaurs had more than 1, 000 teeth.

- Most dinosaur remains have been found in the United States.

Snapper

A camera has been found on the island, and it contains lots of extreme close-ups. Can you piece the snaps together to figure out which dino this visitor saw last?

The dino caught on camera is a

_____

Answer on page 77

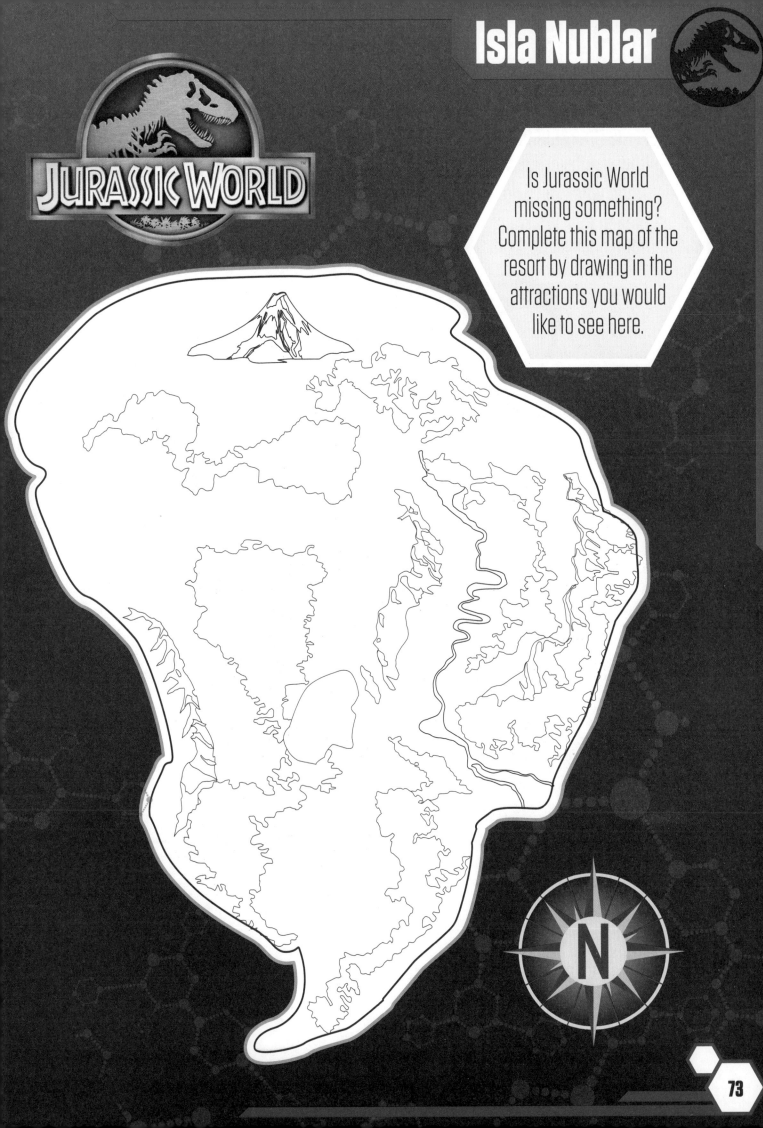

Is Jurassic World missing something? Complete this map of the resort by drawing in the attractions you would like to see here.

The Big Dino Quiz Part 3

In the final section, we want to test how much you know about dinos – and what you'd do if you came face to face with one!

1 What does a Gallimimus eat?

a. Plankton
b. Plants, insects and lizards
c. Large dinosaurs

2 What should you do if you see a T. rex?

a. Hide
b. Wave at it
c. Make a lot of noise to confuse it

3 When was the first Velociraptor fossil discovered?

a. 1823
b. 1923
c. 1723

4 What other name has been used for the Apatosaurus?

a. Longosaurus
b. Demisaurus
c. Brontosaurus

5 Roughly how big is the largest dinosaur egg?

a. Tennis ball
b. Basketball
c. Coconut

6 What is a Dimorphodon?

a. Reptile
b. Amphibian
c. Dinosaur

7 How clever is a Stegosaurus?

a. Not very
b. Quite clever
c. Genius level

8 Where have most dino fossils been found?

a. Europe
b. China
c. America

9 What made the dinosaurs extinct?

a. A meteor
b. An earthquake
c. We don't know

10 Which Jurassic World dinosaur hunts in a team?

a. Velociraptor
b. Triceratops
c. Gallimimus

Now total up your scores from each section of the quiz, add them together and find out how you measure up.

1–10: Armchair amateur

You know a few facts, but you find it hard to remember them all without mixing up the details. Come and spend some time with the dinos in Jurassic World – you'll soon learn lots more about them.

11–20: Keen learner

Not bad! You know some of the more obscure dino facts and you obviously love visiting Jurassic World. Keep coming – we've got plenty more to teach you!

21–30: Dino expert

Wow, you really know your stuff! We're impressed with how much you've learned and how quickly you've memorised tiny details. You'd even have a good chance of surviving a dino attack. Jurassic World needs people like you!

Answers on page 77

Answers

Page 7
Apatosaurus

Page 8
20

Page 9
big
theme park
Apatosaurus
T. rex
Isla Nublar
Mosasurus
lagoon
cretaceous cruise
Gyrosphere
golf course
Costa Rica
Triceratops

Pages 10–11
1.c
2.b
3.c
4.c
5.b
6.b
7.c
8.a
9.b
10.b

Page 13
Shark

Page 25

Pages 26–27
1. B (T. rex)
2. D (Mosasaurus)
3. G (Velociraptor)
4. F (Stegosaurus)
5. H (Gallimimus)
6. E (Indominus rex)
7. C (Pteranodon)
8. A (Triceratops)

Page 29

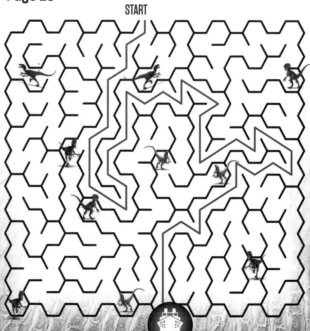

START

FINISH

Page 31

1. Most meat eaters walk on two feet.
2. The Brontosaurus never existed – it was a fossil mix-up!
3. Most dino fossils are found by amateurs.
4. The first dino nest was found in 1923.
5. The largest dino eggs are as big as basketballs.
6. The blue whale is bigger than any dino yet discovered.

Page 41

1. BARYONYX
2. EDMONTOSAURUS
3. MICROCERATUS
4. TRICERATOPS
5. PARASAUROLOPHUS
6. SUCHOMIMUS

Pages 42–43

1. Mosasaurus
2. Ankylosaurus
3. Dimorphodon
4. Stegosaurus
5. Apatosaurus
6. Pteranodon
7. Suchomimus
8. Tyrannosaurus rex
9. Indominus rex
10. Triceratops

Page 53

1. True   2. False   3. False   4. False   5. True
6. False   7. True   8. False   9. True   10. True

Page 66

Page 72

T. rex

Pages 74–75

1. b   2. a   3. b   4. c   5. b
6. a   7. a   8. c   9. c   10. a